The Desiderium Conversations

A.L. REED

INWARDTHOUGHTS

www.inwardthoughts.com

Design and artwork by A.L. REED

Copyright © 2022 A.L. REED

ISBN: 979-8-9874109-0-5

DEDICATION

For my son

CONTENTS

INNOCENCE

"Why can't I see God?" The child asked.

"O my son," the father smiled, "God is not something you see with your eyes, like trees or branches. He is like the wind and the air. He is everywhere."

"But how do we see him?"

"Not with these eyes." He smiled again. "One has to see with this eye." The boy's father gently took his son's hand and guided it to his chest. The child could feel the beating of his father's heart.

"Do you understand now?"

"No, I don't, Daddy!"

Another smile.

Warm light.

"You will understand someday, my son. In fact, you will see God through the yearning that you just expressed. Remember this my child, it is God who sees in you first. Once you understand this, you will see him as well."

The father smiled again and said, "You will indeed see God. I can already see him in you now!"

With curiosity overflowing, the boy basked in the light of his father's words. "This is the talk of grown-ups," he said to himself.

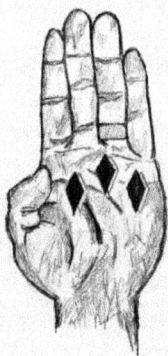

THE PRODIGAL SON

After many years watching his father yearn for his brother's return, Cain became angry.

"Look here, Father. For so many years I have served you, listened to your words and obeyed your instruction. All this time, your other son has only caused you pain and suffering, constantly abandoning you for his whores. Why is it that you continue to look for him night after night? You are wasting away before me, old man. Is there nothing I can do to save you?"

"Save me?" The father looked up.

"My son, have you not learned anything from me, even after all these years? Why should I be angry with my other son whom you say, has abandoned me? In truth I tell you, he has only gone looking for me. Should I not now, also go and look for my lost lamb? Would you rather I praise the hate that stands beside me instead? Is that how you wish to save me?

"*Father*, is it not I who loves you? Is it not I who stands beside you in your pain? How can you say that I oppose you?"

"My son, a man remains what he is no matter where he stands. Man is habitual, and if what he chooses to carry in his heart is darkness, then so shall he be. Listen carefully, Cain. Only after you learn to possess nothing can you begin to possess everything. Let go of your hate, my son! Truly I tell you, anger thrives only when the illusion of control is fed. What do you really grasp of your brother's way, let alone your own? As the ancient ones have said, we are only dust, born from it and destined to return."

"Father, I love you! Why do you say these things when all I seek is to relieve you from your suffering! My anger is just!"

"Justice knows all sides, my son. Anything less

is an imposter! Cannot joy be found in sorrow? Should not joy be found in sorrow? I tell you the truth, everything I have is yours. Everything I have has always been yours – my joy, my sorrow, my riches, my peace – everything has always belonged to you!"

"You speak in riddles, Father! Half your riches you've already gone and wasted on this other son of yours! If you continue like this, you'll have nothing left to give!"

"Is not life more than food and money?"

"Listen to me child, do you remember the story of the feeding of the five thousand?"

"Yes Father."

"What was it that fed the crowds? Was it the boy with the fish? Or was it the Christ to whom the boy gave his fish?"

The father paused before continuing.

"It was the fish that fed the five thousand, Cain! And do you know what the fish was?"

"Speak plainly, Father."

"Behold Cain, the fish was all those who chose to partake in the miracle. The fish was of course, the Christ himself. But the fish was also the boy. The fish was the poor, the dispirited, and all those who were hungry. All these became the fish, my child. The fish who fed all, became a part of all who were willing to participate. And so, I say to you again, everything I have is yours. Receive this and remember, a man is ultimately what he chooses to dwell upon, and a family is all those to whom it accepts."

"Father! Your rhetoric makes me equal to my brother. Can you not see this?! All is not equal! Consider again how I, and I alone, have served you faithfully. It is I that has stood by your side, and I who has done all that you have asked. Am I to dine at my brother's table? Are we to be served the same lot? I cannot accept this!"

"Behold, I am the fish, Cain! And so too have you been called. Wake up and take part in me! We are broken bread for the birds. Wine poured out to nourish the thirsty. Although you stand before me now in body, like your brother, you have also been searching for me in other lands. You too have lost your way. You too have hated me along the journey, and I have disappointed you! I know this! I have not been what you expected, but I remain what I am! I stand before you now with open arms to receive you home. Stop grasping at your godlikeness. To do so makes you nothing like God. Let go of yourself and yearn for me. Fall to the ground like seed for the birds. Let all the rich, the poor, everyone eat and drink of what I will fill you with, so that you too might be the source of eternal life."

The father stopped, put his hands on his son's shoulders and looked directly into his eyes.

"Find life Cain, by yearning for your brother! Yearn for his restoration. See, taste, and smell the goodness that is ever present around you. I was born to give life, and to give it in abundance. You have misunderstood this abundance and looked to fill your cup elsewhere, just like your brother. Empty your cup, Cain! It is full of selfish expectations and false promises. Remember, all that does not come from me will let you down. Empty your cup, Cain, and I will fill you up like I did the five thousand. I will turn you into fine wine, and you will overflow to the masses beside you.

Empty your cup so that you can drink of my abundance. Empty your cup, so that all can drink of my abundance."

As the father finished saying these words, Cain's countenance changed. Raising a trembling hand, he pointed to a shadow in the distance. The father immediately recognized his lost son and raced out to embrace him. As the old man ran with his arms stretched out, the lost son beheld his father's face. It was his own. All his yearning, all his wrestling, all his suffering – it was nothing other than all his father's yearning, his father's wrestling, and his father's suffering for him. They embraced. The sons wept.

THE THIEF ON THE CROSS

"*Who are you?*"   The thief on the cross demanded. Spit sprayed from his mouth. "Are you Rama, Krishna, the Buddha?"

The air was hot and thick, stained with the odor of sweat and blood. The rabid thief glared at the man beside him.

The response that came was quiet and gentle.

"Who do I need to be? Who do I need to be so that you will yearn for me? I am who I am."

"*Brother!*"   A second thief suddenly cried out. "Stop harassing him! You and I belong here! This man's done nothing wrong, though! He is innocent! I've heard his teachings myself, and he speaks truth!"

"*What is truth?*" Came the sharp reply.

"We were only children when father was robbed, beaten, and left for dead! Do you not remember, Cain? Father would have lived if it were not for the holy fools, such as this one, stepping over him again and again. Could his blood really have stained their purity? We are only here because of men like this! *This* man's truth not only robbed us of our father's life, but of our innocence as well! *What is God that man should be mindful of him?*"

The reply from the man beside was again, kind and tender.

"Let wisdom be vindicated by her deeds."

He paused.

"Abel, pour your brokenness into my innocence, and I will pour my innocence into your brokenness."

After saying this, the man turned his gaze upon the crowd and spoke to them saying,

"Behold, I desire no effort other than mercy! I have made you all a little lower than the gods so that you might shine like diamonds on the sea! How long will you go on filling your bowls with food that cannot satisfy your hunger? How long will you continue to fill your bellies with misplaced identity and the illusion of control? How long will you reject your neighbor, whose face indeed shines God, if not more than your own? All you who have ears to hear, you are intended manifestations of my glory, my beauty, and wonder! You are conduits of grace and peace, extensions of God's mercy. Arise now and take part in my bringing about the restoration and unity of all things! You are the salt of the world, and light upon these hills! You are my promise that I have not forgotten, or abandoned this world, but am here in this world! Your lives have always been the prayer of my life. Now take up your mats, go and make my life the prayer of yours."

After saying these things, he turned his gaze back upon Abel and said,

"Today, you and your brother will be with me in paradise."

Upon hearing this, the crowds were astonished, saying to themselves, "Who is this man, that even those who spit upon him are loved and called manifestations of his glory?"

THE RECONCILIATION

"I've finally found you!" The disheveled priest cried out while struggling into the small room and awkwardly seating himself next to the man on the bed.

"Will you ever forgive me?" He choked on the words. His body quivered as he leaned over the dying man with his hands pressed together. "Will you ever forgive me for walking past you on the road?" He whispered.

The man on the bed, badly beaten and wrapped in bandages, looked up and gazed quietly at his visitor. His eyes were in another place; they were from another place.

"I am sorry. I am so sorry! Nothing about my

journey justified leaving you on the road. I am ashamed for leaving you, my neighbor. You were my brother in need, and I ignored you. I told myself that there would be another that would pass by and help you. I told myself that you would be okay, and that I didn't need to be there, but... O God! There was another man!"

The realization suddenly struck the priest.

"A good man brought you here. Yes? He paid to have you bandaged and cared for. He acted as your true neighbor!"

"O God!" The priest moved down to his knees. "Forgive me! My heart burned for you, it truly did. My conscience kept pulling me back towards you. In my mind, I continued with excuse after excuse, but I knew that you were calling me back."

The priest paused.

"I didn't want to be interrupted. I had places to go, places to be, and I forgot – I forgot."

There was a long silence, and many minutes passed before the priest slowly stood up. His eyes were shining.

"My God! I forgot who I was! I forgot why I was created. Never in my life have I been my own. I have always belonged to all!"

The priest remembered his place.

He reached down and grasped the dying man's hand.

The pearl.

Grace and forgiveness danced in his mind, and he fell back to his knees. He gazed into the dying man's eyes.

There was silence.

Emptiness.

"All this suffering because of me!" The priest said, whispering again. "You suffer because of me, and now you forgive me!?"

Tears fell from both men.

The man on the bed took his last breath.

The priest leaned over and kissed his forehead.

He said, "Father, thank you for hearing me. Thank you for loving me."

CAIN AND ABEL

In the cool of the morning with dew still on the grass, a man began to weep, a deer looked up, and a fox ran off into the woods.

"Why do you cry?"

"Brother, I have lost my way."

"Have you not heard that light shines brightest in the dark?"

"How can the dead speak like this?"

"It is time to stop grasping for the past, my brother. Let your eyes fall upon that which rests before you now. Behold! Look at what your tears are watering this very moment!"

Cain looked down at the color reaching out from the ground.

"Brother, I do not understand. Even seeing the beauty of these flowers, I cannot erase the suffering that I've caused! I've destroyed our family, done what is unforgiveable. What else should my tears be seeking, if not that very place from which you are speaking?"

"O Cain! You only see in part! These flowers that cover my grave are your reminder that beauty covers over everything. Can you not see that you too are one of these little flowers? You have forgotten what you are, and only identified yourself as the death below. You are also life, Cain. Continually becoming. You exist because of love, and you will continue to exist because of love. Therefore, arise!

"How can you speak to me like this, when everything around us continues to reek of the death I brought forth upon our family? The suffering I hold is overwhelming, and any thirst for life, or hope for future restoration, has long since passed!"

"The beauty which you long for is still shining inside you. Look at how your tears sparkle. Streams of living water pour out from your lantern. Indeed, it is true that you have peered into the void and dined with death. But take heart, open your eyes. See too, that this death is just another step on the ladder of life. All this trouble of yours, all this suffering, it's about calling you home. You still exist, Cain! The river is still running. Mercy has been provided. Look up and let the infinite sky of God's compassion embrace you. Yearn for him as you see nature yearn. Nothing is unforgivable! Press yourself back into the vine, my struggling branch! Be infused by the beauty that transcends everything. Chase your tears into this soil that desires to nourish you. Reach towards this light, and long for it with every cell in your body, and you will be changed."

Upon hearing these words, Cain stopped his weeping. "Brother," he said, "I do not know if I will ever be able to see as you do."

And then he looked up, and there was light shining through the trees. The deer began to graze again, and the fox never returned.

LACRIMOSA

As the stranger approached the well, the boy stooped down and began to write in the dirt. Knowing the boy's thoughts, the stranger looked at him and said, "I tell you the truth child, before this day began, I saw you sitting here by this well. I will tell you my story, as your heart has desired, if you will only draw me some water and allow me to rest for a moment."

With curiosity overflowing, the boy replied, "Sir, I can see that you are a prophet, and that you have many things to share. Indeed, I will draw you some water if, as you promised, you will share your story."

The man stooped down, adjusted his sandals,

and smiled.

"I am no prophet, my boy. My name is Abel, and I have been a wanderer in these lands for many years. I once even stood in this very place. I was a different man at that time. I was an angry man, but there was girl who helped me."

The traveler paused and looked away for a moment.

"God, she was beautiful," he whispered to himself.

"The girl kindly gave me water, as you also just did for me now. She asked how I had come to find myself at her well, and I told her about all my suffering, how I had once been a rich man, and in want of nothing. I had been the most desirable merchant in the land, until it all came to an end. My family had been destroyed by a fire, and my body afterwards was ravaged by disease. For years I wasted away in the desert, giving myself over to drink and scraping myself with rocks. One day, knowing that death was near, I decided to go back to my village. I thought that maybe by returning home, some sliver of hope might still be found, and my life be restored."

"After the girl handed me her cup of water, she looked at me strangely and said,

'Sir, this water I give you will never be able to quench your thirst, just as your previous life could never have quenched your thirst. You must thirst for something more. You must be restless for something more. Only then can you find the restoration that you long for.'

"What is this restoration that you speak of my child? I am near death! Please give me what you have and save me from the darkness that overwhelms my soul."

"'Let me speak to your father.' The girl said to me."

"That's absurd! Have you not listened to anything I've said!? My father was lost in the fire!"

'You are almost correct, Sir. You lost one of your fathers in the fire. You still have many fathers to lose!'

"The girl said this to me, and I understood at once."

The traveler stopped speaking and looked carefully at the boy.

"Do you understand what I have been saying, my boy?"

The boy had understood.

The traveler's words had satisfied what the boy had been longing for, and with no further need of his father's words, the boy turned and made his way into the desert.

THE MAN WITH NO TALENTS

Before the master left on his long journey, he called his servant and entrusted him with a large quantity of talents to manage and care for his kingdom. The servant bowed low, and humbly accepted the amount provided. With good intention and a deep love for his master's way, the servant set about keeping order to the property, even seeking to increase its value.

It wasn't long however, that the servant found himself facing difficult seasons, bad harvests, and clever thieves. Soon he was struggling. He had no more talents to purchase the goods necessary for running the kingdom. He could no longer pay the workers in the field, and he could no longer feed any of the animals properly. Even the portion of talents that he had invested for kingdom growth and security, were now gone. The servant was utterly bankrupt. He no longer had the means to care for his master's property, and was eventually forced to sell everything remaining, just to maintain rights to the land.

When the master finally returned, he found his servant in the field, alone and ashamed. The servant looked up, beheld his master's face, and began to weep.

"Master, I have failed you. I have lost the talents you gave me. I have lost everything that you entrusted me, except for this field. I am ashamed to be called your servant, and I can understand if you wish to banish me from your sight forever."

The master stepped down from his horse and put his strong hands on the servant's shoulders. The servant would not look up, but he listened to his master's voice.

"My Child, many of the workers in my vineyard grumbled because they were only here for talents. If their eyes had been open, they would have seen that just being in my vineyard at all was the glory! You, on the other hand, have yearned to remain in my kingdom, not for talents, but purely because of your love for me."

The servant looked up at the master. The master continued.

"I have given you everything because you have given me everything. And what I have given you, you can never lose. Up until now, you have only seen in part, but now you will see in full. Now is the time to join me in my departure for other lands. The results of your efforts here were never the purpose. What happened to my talents entrusted you was never my true concern. I am the shepherd, and you are my lamb. Here we are, the lamb that I have longed for, and the lamb that has longed for me. This is all that I have ever asked, and all that you could have ever provided. And look now how you stand in this empty field! Bravo! Well done my good and faithful servant!"

The servant basked in the light of his master's words. Grace danced in his heart, and he embraced that which had always been with him, that which had never forsaken him.

OSTRICH CRUMBS

"Why do you continue to follow me?" The farmer kindly asked the large bird trailing along behind him.

The ostrich, which had shown up at his door some weeks earlier, continued to meet him every morning after that first visit.

The bird would follow the farmer up the road and wait for seeds to fall from his sack; seeds that he carried up each day for his other animals. Every time some seed would fall, the ostrich would run and quickly snatch it up. Evidently pleased by what was received, the ostrich would run circles around the farmer, doing his best to show appreciation.

The farmer, always gracious, never chased the bird away, nor offered any more than what the small holes in the sack provided. Day after day this went on until one morning, the farmer unexpectedly emerged from his house without his sack of seeds.

The ostrich, noticeably puzzled, still followed the farmer up the road. Finally, at the barn, the farmer stopped and seated himself on a stack of hay. He looked directly at the bird and said, "It is now time for you to speak, my consistent friend." The farmer continued. "Why is it that you continue to follow me day after day? What is it that you are looking for?"

The bird's mouth was immediately opened, and he said to the farmer,

"Good farmer, I know that I am not one of your barn animals, but after meeting you, and experiencing your great compassion, I could not help but continue to follow you. You have provided crumbs to this poor bird each morning, and these crumbs have been sufficient for me. Please, good farmer, lest these seeds continue to fall to the ground, I see now that I will die. Will you continue to nourish me with these crumbs?"

"Dear Ostrich, I will give you these crumbs and more!" And with these words, the farmer proceeded to feed his bird:

Behold, I am here to wake you up and give you life!"

❧

We are all diamonds. Every one of us, precious
jewels worthy of pursuit.

❧

Opening the doors to your house will allow the wind to blow inside.

Extinguish the flame with your fingers and you risk burning your hand. Use your breath instead and behold how the mountains will move. Leave your efforts behind.

I gave up being smart a long time ago so that I could spend more time laughing with God.

☙

As water seeks out the path of least resistance, so God expresses himself in those who are least resistant.

☙

If a man's actions can convince one of evil, then so too should a man's actions convince one of God.

It is good to give up the illusion of control, but even better to give up the illusion that everything is out of control.

Life is like chasing your shadow. The faster you move, the faster it will move. If you slow down, it too will slow down.

I thank God every cold night for removing my blanket of religion.

❧

I do not choose who eats the fruit from my branches. Nor should I.

❧

✦

I say what has already been said, and I manifest that which has already been manifested. We are all ships carrying the same cargo, glasses holding the same wine. Some will drink from my well, and others will drink from other wells. What matters in the end, is that God is being given.

✦

How can one have eyes to see if there is no desire to look? Ask yourself therefore, what you yearn for before you decide to knock. Many will wish to know, but few will really ask.

❧

Does the wind pick up and carry away large rocks? No. It picks up and carries away dry and brittle leaves, sweet pollen from flowers, and all those other elements weighing no more than a feather. Listen carefully, the spirit will raise up many kinds of things, but what is common among them all, is that they carry little weight. It's time to drop your bags, little children. Stop holding on to whatever you think is grounding you. It's all going to be carried away in the end anyway. Why not make it you now?

❧

Man's fundamental problem is his desire to rule nature, his desire to be God. The Tower of Babel was nothing other than a physical manifestation of this ongoing problem of the heart. God has never been worried about us building ourselves up to Him, He's been saving us from building ourselves into Him.

Yearning is the spaceship that shoots us out of this world and into the larger galaxy of perception. We lose our words in silence, we lose our weight in space. We consider new hope in distant planets, and we encounter new light in deeper darkness.

❦

Love, hope, beauty, and life are personified through the Christ who descends like a falling leaf into the world's brokenness. Find life by letting go. Fall to the ground. Like water cuts through rock when descending to lower places, or the mustard seed fits through the eye of a needle, faith is yielding. Hope is yearning.

❦

It is precisely because roads bend that we encounter new perspectives. Therefore, pick up your bags my friends, and travel wisely your crooked paths.

❧

Can anyone hold hands with one who isn't present? Think about it. It was for this reason that Jesus was born poor. The father sent his son into the world, to take hold of our poor hands, to adopt us into his kingdom, to be reborn into poverty, to take hold of poor hands, to adopt into his kingdom, to be reborn into poverty, to take hold of poor hands, to adopt into his kingdom, etc. Because that is what love does, it extends itself into oblivion.

❧

Each life is a moment. Each moment should
be cherished. A flash of divine light. An
incarnation. I am an incarnation too. I am
with you for a little while. A French horn. I
will play my notes and then I will go. Will you
listen?

❦

I am a part of nature! A walking tree, I provide you relief from a blinding sun. Take a moment and let your eyes adjust a little in my shade. Enjoy some cool air before the real shining takes place. It's going to get hot, my friends! Maybe I can help you prepare a little beforehand.

❦

I am just another lamp with two purposes. To be plugged in, and to provide light to those of you in my room.

As the eye is the lamp of the body, how we choose to perceive the world will be the root wick of our existence.

Where we choose to invest our heart will determine how we sprout and whether the kingdom inside us will bloom.

♦

Seasons speak a truth to all of us that life is change. Summers lead to winters, which return to summers. In one moment, our families are close and connected, and in another, they're distant and broken. Children grow older and choose different paths, sometimes good, and sometimes painful. Parents grow older and along with imparting learned wisdom, spend time in hospitals for tired hearts and dementia. Fun and games played in holiday wind, soon carries off friends and family to distant cities and states. Love and joy in relationships swing into heartbreak, which often return to love and joy. Like rain from passing clouds fall only for a time, so money comes and goes, giving comfort and then taking it back again. One day our loved ones are healthy, and the next day they are not. One day we pray for a loved one, and the next day we do not. One day we pray for a cancer patient, and the next day we are the cancer patient. All the while, dear God carries us up like the dried leaves in an autumn breeze. In the warmth of His sun, He builds character reflected in the dry and brittleness of our once naïve, green leaves. What should we learn through all this? That life is change. Rather than always looking forward to the next moment and letting life pass us by, take hold of every moment. Be in it.

🔖

🔖

What does it mean to exist? I know not. I feel myself shine though. I experience beats of time, standing alone and embracing all. The feeling is fresh like water. Splash! Flowers bloom. Grassy breeze drifts down through the mind's open doors. The scent is soft. Tender movements feel through air. Her hair is wrapped around our bodies close. Life shines through. Gold rings. Washed clean. Beauty's beam. Existence shines.

🔖

Where is God?
I have found him.
He is in suffering.
He came to me.

The religious person spends too much time
looking at the faults of others rather than
looking at the faults within.
All men are the religious person in one way or
another.
The religious person thinks it is others who
are sick.
All men deceive themselves when they know
something that makes them better than
others.
The religious person is only awake in sleep.
All men are awake when they contemplate.

❦

Religion is often pushed on us like a new pair of shoes, squeaky clean and polished. The truth is, one doesn't really know anything about God until one's shoes are broken in, worn out and stained. It's the first dent in the car, the cracks in the pavement. God in us hurts. It's not what we expect, and don't let anybody tell you otherwise.

❦

Today I went to the park where I rested in a tree's arms and contemplated the meaning of life. The sun's light was around the leaves.

Rusty, rising sun, scratch this morning sky and flood this dark city with golden hue. Raise up your children of light with eyes wide open and hearts filled with transcendent grace. Wish me well east wind. Groom your waters, for I will travel their chilly darkness with hope-born courage and mindful peace.

❦

Let's stop working this out as just another problem to solve, or a belief to defend. Stand back and consider the system, my friend. Why does the sound ring so stale? How does everyone know so well? I don't. Let's stop pretending. Let's stop fooling. No denial here. Surely, I can't take another linguistic pot of tea. I am tea full. And was that all I was meant to be, just another pot of tea? O please. There must be more.

❦

❧

Isn't it interesting that as soon as someone thinks they are interesting, they become the most uninteresting? And isn't it interesting that when someone thinks they are uninteresting, they often become very interesting? But who really thinks anyone continues to be interesting or uninteresting? After all, don't we ourselves continue to fluctuate between being interesting and uninteresting?

❧

❦

Quiet road winds through hills with windshield wipers wetting windows. Wet glass. Met tasks. Mist sits waiting on silent past. Shadowed trees and bending willows watching closely the moving meadows. There are no cars here on this winding road, this quiet ghetto.

❦

Krishna, you finite form of the infinite! O how you proclaim Jesus! Kongzi, are not your ways and reflections those of the Jews? Beautiful Zen, teacher of peace and abandonment, do you not prepare me for personal acquaintance with my savior, Jesus Christ? Lao-Tzu, Plato, Camus, and Nietzsche, thank you for all your insight, your thoughts and honesty. All bleed truth. Darkness embraced by light. This poetry. This life. This gift. Revelation beyond the Book. Happiness. Joy. Peace. O God beyond understanding, my God of grace. Jesus! Teach us all to see your perfect forgiveness. You love in authentic, open, and empty contemplation.

❧

O blessed suffering! You bleed tears of liberation, need for reformation, and hope for restoration. I've found Christian grace! Ah, forgiving space where life springs forth flowers of effortless course. Cleanse these thoughts with empty bowls of mercy meadows. A scented nirvana glowing pearls of peace and holy souls that forever shine in cool caves of restful union. Release this life and be filled with Christ. With light. With love.

❧

Living flame of love and embracer of all, you are a most graceful friend. Calming the anxious and providing rapture to hate, you are a compassionate mystery. Blesser of misery, your sparkling waters of peace transcend all Karma. Personified Zen, you are beautiful dove come quiet and filling all hearts. Teach us your music, O lover and light of the world!

While the masses call it a feeling and the religious call it a dying, we all seem to be missing an important aspect about the path to love. It is the way of giving and receiving. Surely feelings, in and of themselves, are a footwear less likely to carry us down the path to love, than is the concept of service and self-sacrifice. After all, love is only alive in a context where feelings are born from energies invested. But service and self-sacrifice left on their own, will surely only end in anger and bitterness (a bankrupt form of travel, as well). To pursue a life of giving for giving's sake, or feeling for feeling's sake, is not enough. To be in the garden of love is to walk a circular path of giving *and* receiving. How can a relationship truly thrive without receiving what has been given, and giving what has been received? There must be both!

A great mystery of the divine is that there is both unity and plurality. In the Christian tradition, God is three persons existing in a unity of love, three persons taking care of each other eternally through giving and receiving. In this sense, the world has never been restricted of love. It has always been in love.

☀

Infinite love, by its very nature it is an attribute that seeks extension. Behold that there even be such a thing as love. In this alone, we have reason for why there exists something rather than nothing.

☀

❧

As channels of divine love, we are by design, blessed through the blessing of others. We are conduits where the good that others receive, is merely a manifestation of that which is already flowing through us. We love because He first loved us.

❧

✷

Divinity suffers too. No longer abstract. No longer separate. Heaven participates in pain. Bring your ladle to his well. Dip into his darkness. Climb into his overwhelming compassion, his confronting love, his sufficient mercy. Glassy mirror, problematic existence parts the way. So long misery!

✷

Transcend your sin through obedience to the body. Pursue the course and follow its methods. Soon you will find that even this must be transcended. Wonder. God is no book. God is no group. God is beyond all and giving all. Beyond and quiet, He is love in fragrant violet. He is pure being, part of all and inviting all. Transcendent voice calling into the abyss, Jesus please one day raise us all into your eternal kiss.

❦

Why Jesus? Because only he came out to find me. In mercy he came acknowledging, answering deep despair and darkness. While all was not well, he showed me Tao. Light in darkness. Reconciling the angel and insect. I will leave it all for this beauty, this wonderful grace in the night.

❦

Beautiful God, my cycle of death and rebirth flows through you. Completely empty, I am filled with you. Even after death, I am again made holy by you. In winter you strip my leaves from me, but you sustain the leaf because I am planted by streams of water. I have hated you and I have loved you. You are the only that has remained constant. You are that from which I would be nothing. In you I am everything. I was born to die and in death I live, as you have lived for me. I will continue to die again and again. This is my path.

❖

What's not to say? The cool of day is blue. Green zipline me away into soft ends of flower fields and drizzle mornings. I am happy high now, this guy. Gray showers have parted way. Nothing left but bubbly stars and me standing nowhere. I am nowhere and happy to say, "what's not to say?"

❖

Daughter. Divine. Light and breasts. Mood stirs stars. Peace and rest. Hope. Days. Full of life. Shine forever. Pleased to meet you, Destiny.

Divinity kisses me in her moonlight wanderings. She is my music. My life in morning grace.

❧

Live in everyone's moment. Step out of yourself and take a deep breath. Breath in every sound around you, every scent, laugh, tear, mistake, cough, cry. Every movement. Look at the entire tree and remember that you are just one rustling leave among thousands. The beauty is in the rustling, and the sun shining through, and that we even get to participate! O my God!! This is overwhelming!

❧

❦

I hate my noisy sprinkler system. It always wakes me up in the night. And while we are on the subject, I don't like talking about sin. It always wakes me up to my hypocrisy. There's just too much noise in this world. What on earth are you up to, God? Can you turn it down please! Don't you know I need my beauty sleep!

Then, the Lord looked at me and said, "Has the old wine really been good enough? Why have you been crying for my presence all this time, only to reject it once it surrounds you? What is this ungrateful attitude now that I have shown myself? The party has just begun!"

Then the master said to his guards, "Throw this man out with the other sleepers! Go and find some people who really want to party!"

❦

Every movement, every word is a
manifestation of where we've made our home.

❧

Take off your clothes before trying to swim in the river of God!

❧

Can a man with no knowledge, move into the wilderness and expect to live? Neither should one seek to understand God without expecting to die.

We are not just a total of our own life decisions and experiences; we are a sum of everyone's life decisions and experiences. We are an interconnected web of everyone.

※

God does not see us for that which we are not, He sees us for that which we are becoming.

※

THE GREAT PEARL

"Brother, I had a dream the other night."

"Can you tell me about it?"

"I was standing in an empty house at the top of a large hill. There was nothing inside the house except curtains hanging over the windows. They were dancing wild because of a strong wind, and I was sitting on the floor alone, waiting for something."

"What were you waiting for?"

"It wasn't revealed, but I was excited. I went outside and looked down the hill to see if I might catch a glimpse of what was causing my excitement."

"And what did you see?"

"I saw an ocean below, and thousands of people pouring out of great ships. The crowds were everywhere, and they were all making their way towards my house up a narrow road."

"What did you do?"

"I was overwhelmed. I quickly went back to my house and stood in the doorway, doing my best to prepare for their arrival."

"And then what happened?"

"Well, after a few minutes they did begin to arrive. I immediately recognized the first who appeared. They were old friends from my childhood. Then, as more people began to make their way over the hill, I began to understand that there were none of whom I did not know. They were all friends, family, even people I had only met one or two times in my life."

"Was the experience good?"

"Oh yes! Everyone was smiling. I too was

smiling. There was a mysterious presence of joy and happiness, and it swirled around everyone. It seemed to pour out of everything. No one would enter my house without first greeting me at the door. Some shook my hand, and others embraced me. Some cried, and some laughed. It was perfect, my brother! It was beautiful!"

"And was that the end of the dream?"

"Oh no! It was then that I met the man standing beside me. When I looked at his face, it contained all the faces of everybody I have ever known. I don't think I can explain it better than that.

'I am the great pearl,' he said to me. 'I am the great pearl beside you, the great pearl within you, the great pearls around you. Always shining.'

And then I opened my eyes."

INNOCENCE REBORN

"Why can't I see God?" the child asked.

"O my son," the boy's father smiled, "God is not something you see with your eyes, like trees or branches. He is like the wind and the air. He is everywhere."

"But how do we see him?"

"I tell you the truth," his father smiled. "If you have seen me, you have seen God!" The boy's father gently took his son's hand and guided it to his chest. The boy could feel the beating of his father's heart.

"Do you understand now, my child?"

ABOUT THE AUTHOR

I am a person of you
And you this person free
Though we be one in humanity
Just like those notes amongst a harmony